SPALDING
BASKETBALL
Playbook
Plays from the Pros

MASTERS PRESS

A DIVISION OF HOWARD W. SAMS & CO.

Published by Masters Press
(A Division of Howard W. Sams & Co.)
2647 Waterfront Pkwy. E. Drive, Suite 300
Indianapolis, IN 46214

Library of Congress Cataloging-in-Publication Data

Ociepka, Bob, 1948-
    Basketball playbook: plays from the pros / Bob Ociepka & Dale Ratermann.
        p.   cm.
    At head of title: Spalding
    ISBN 1-57028-008-8 (pbk.)
    1. Basketball--Offense. 2. Basketball--Coaching. 3. National Basketball Association. I. Ratermann, Dale, 1956-   . II. Title.
GV889.034   1995   95-7520
796.323'2--dc20   CIP

ACKNOWLEDGMENTS

To enter any profession requires someone to have enough confidence in you to give you a chance — to give you a start. I was extremely fortunate to have someone give me not one, but two starts: Dick Versace. Dick hired me out of college and gave me my first coaching job at Gordon Tech High School in Chicago in 1970. He then gave me my first job in the National Basketball Association with the Indiana Pacers in 1989. He immediately motivated me to make coaching my life's work and over the years has remained a close friend, as well as a colleague.

I am grateful to athletic directors Tom Winiecki and Jack Tosh, who believed in me and allowed me to run their high school programs. They gave me the opportunity to grow as a coach and helped develop the foundation which led to the chance to advance to the NBA.

I have learned more than just basketball from Bob Hill, Bob Weiss and Bill Fitch, the other three coaches I have worked for in the NBA. They all have given me the chance to remain part of a rather exclusive club, and I am very grateful to each of them.

Finally, a special thanks to all the NBA coaches whose work appears in this book. Without their efforts, none of this would be possible.

—B.O.

The authors would like to thank all of the NBA's public relations directors who have contributed photographs, as well as these people from Masters Press:
Holly Kondras, Managing Editor
Heather Seal, Editor
Pat Brady, Proofreader
Phil Velikan and Lynne Clark, Cover Design
Christy Pierce, Diagrams
Terry Varvel, Production Assistance

—B.O. and D.R.

TABLE OF CONTENTS

INTRODUCTION

Dr. James Naismith introduced basketball to his class at the Springfield, Mass., YMCA at 10 a.m. on a winter day in 1891. Legend has it that at 10:03 someone already was diagramming the pick-and-roll, using the peaches that came with the peach basket.

At all levels of basketball — from grade school intramurals to the National Basketball Association — plays are diagrammed. They might be drawn on the dressing room chalkboard, a clipboard in the huddle or in the dirt next to an asphalt court. But everyone who answers to the name "Coach" spends time with X's and O's.

In the NBA, there are a number of plays used by nearly every team. Coaches slightly adjust the plays to best fit their personnel. Even though today's players are bigger and faster, and the tempo of the game is quicker, most of the modern plays are only adaptations of successful sets that have been around for years.

It's been said: "If you steal from one source, it's plagiarism. If you steal from a lot of sources, it's research." Good basketball coaches do lots of research. Many of the plays that are successful on the highest level of the game also can be successful on other levels.

The offensive plays detailed in this book are used in the NBA by a number of teams. They were selected to provide a sampling from some of the most successful coaches and teams. The plays are titled using common NBA terminology and are presented from an NBA scout's viewpoint. Teaching points and nuances of plays can be determined only by being at a coach's practice sessions or in the huddle. And successful coaches continuously tweak plays.

It is hoped that a coach on any level can utilize this book to select plays which will fit a particular style and system. Each can be adapted to provide scoring opportunities for the best players on any team.

But remember, each play is appropriate only if it fits the team's personnel. A play that the New York Knicks' Pat Riley uses to get a post-up for Patrick Ewing will not be successful on the high school level if your 6-foot-2 sophomore center is being guarded by a 6-foot-10 Division I prospect.

However, that 6-foot-2 center could be used out on the floor (pulling the 6-foot-10 phenom away from the basket) to set screens similar to what Lenny Wilkens utilizes with the Atlanta Hawks on a baseline out-of-bounds play.

Although each play is designed to get a specific player a shot at the basket, all properly conceived plays have more than one option. So, a play that is drawn up to create a shot for the shooting guard must have secondary options which will create opportunities for other players if the initial action is stopped. If a play is designed with only one player in mind, there is a tendency for the other players on the court to let down and perhaps not carry out their assignments. A good coach designs plays that have the initial thrust of getting a specific player a shot, but also involve all five players on the court.

Positions

For simplicity, the court diagrams are numbered according to positions:

1 = Point Guard

Throughout the NBA, there are different types of point guards with very different skills, strengths and weaknesses. Every point guard on every team at every level brings something unique to the court. The point guard is the primary ball handler and the floor general. But the point guard might be a penetrator, shooter or set-up man. It is important that the offense takes into account the strengths of its point guard. The offense starts here.

Examples: Magic Johnson, Isiah Thomas, Kevin Johnson, Muggsy Bogues, Kenny Anderson, John Stockton.

2 = Shooting Guard

Normally, coaches prefer the "2-man" to have good shooting range and an ability to come off screens and hit jump shots. Coaches prefer this player to have skills to drive the ball to the basket when the jump shot is taken away by the defense. With the advent of the three-point shot, it helps if this player can consistently hit from that distance. This allows a team to stretch a defense (keeping them from sagging in and helping on inside players).

Examples: Michael Jordan, Reggie Miller, Joe Dumars, Clyde Drexler, Jeff Hornacek, Mitch Richmond, Vern Maxwell.

3 = *Small Forward*

This is a combination skill position, because the ideal "3-man" is expected to be able to shoot from the outside, drive to the basket and post-up. Most of the small forwards in the NBA cannot do all three things well. The better ones are able to do at least two of them. Coaches also want a player who can go to the offensive board.

Examples: Scottie Pippen, Dominique Wilkins, Danny Manning, Detlef Schrempf, Glen Rice, Jamal Mashburn.

4 = *Power Forward*

The power forward usually is a low-post player who is a good rebounder. Some teams use a smaller "4-man" and play him outside to drive against bigger defenders. But generally, a power forward is the second biggest player in the line-up who does a lot of dirty work around the basket. It helps if he is a good screener who is willing to put his body on people to free teammates for shots.

Examples: Buck Williams, Horace Grant, Charles Barkley, Larry Johnson, Karl Malone, Shawn Kemp, Brian Grant, Vin Baker.

5 = *Center*

The center is usually the primary low-post scorer who can force other teams to double-team him to stop him from scoring inside. Some teams have centers who are not dominant players with their backs to the basket. Coaches will use this type of player to play out on the court, facing the basket, and try to draw the defensive center away from the lane. The best centers can score inside or out and are capable passers and screeners. And a center who also can get a lot of second-shot opportunities for his team will be a certain all-star.

Examples: Hakeem Olajuwon, Patrick Ewing, David Robinson, Shaquille O'Neal, Dikembe Mutombo, Rik Smits.

Each name listed at each position has unique skills. That uniqueness means that plays that look very similar on paper, look very different when they are executed on the court.

NBA teams adjust their offensive systems to accommodate the strengths they possess. Coaches at every level must do the same. A good, honest evaluation of your team should be Step 1. The selection of an offensive system (running style, half-court style, passing game, set offense, etc.) should be Step 2.

The plays in this book were chosen to assist a coach after the first two steps have been taken. And by no means should any team at any level attempt to add all of these plays to its playbook. Find a handful of plays that works for your particular situation and then practice them. Once they can be executed in practice, try them in a game. And then run them again, and again and again. Remember, it's the execution of plays that wins ball games, not the number of plays executed.

SYMBOLS USED IN THE DIAGRAMS

1　**Point Guard**

2　**Shooting Guard**

3　**Small Forward**

4　**Power Forward**

5　**Center**

‹ - -　Direction of pass

=　Handoff

↙　Player's movement

⊢　Screen

○　Player with the ball

⋏⋏⁷　Dribble

"OR"　Player has the option of doing one or the other

To make the diagrams easier to read, a number of court markings (three-point arc, extended NBA free-throw lane, lane markings and hashmarks) have been omitted, except when they are essential to a particular play. Coaches can adjust the plays to fit the court markings of their particular level of competition.

Chapter 1
EARLY OFFENSE PLAYS

Seattle's Loop

Many teams in the NBA run an "early offense" or "quick" set. That occurs when the ball is pushed up the court quickly after a field goal or made free throw. Rather than a free-lance fast break, early offenses are structured plays that take advantage of an opposing team that may be slow setting up its defense.

Seattle Sonics Coach George Karl utilizes this play to bring 2-man Kendall Gill off staggered screens for a jump shot.

In Figure 1, 1 pushes the ball quickly up the right side after 2 (Gill) has sprinted up the right side and 3 up the left side. Player 3 clears across the lane to the right corner as 2 "loops" to the top off staggered screens set by 5 and 4. (If the 4-man inbounds the ball after the basket, then 5 will set the first screen. If 5 inbounds the ball, 4 sets the first screen.) Player 1 passes to 2 at the top of the key.

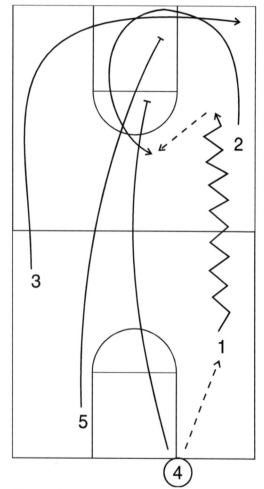

Figure 1

San Antonio's Quick (2-5 Back Screen)

San Antonio Spurs Coach Bob Hill ran this quick play when he was the head coach at Indiana, and now he runs it with the Spurs. For San Antonio, it often results in a lob pass and dunk for David Robinson.

The action begins the same as the previous loop play (Figure 1), except that the 4 and 5 positions are interchanged and 4 sets the first screen for 2. In Figure 2, instead of receiving the second staggered screen from 5, 2 sets a back screen for 5. Player 1 looks to throw the lob pass to 5 (Robinson) or he can pass to 2 who pops out after setting his back screen.

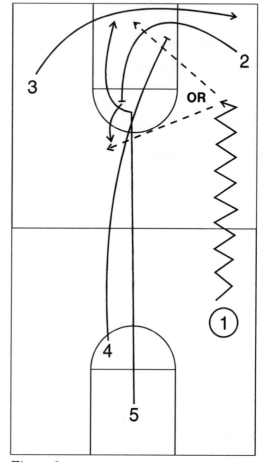

Figure 2

San Antonio Head Coach Bob Hill

Indiana's Quick (1-5 Back Screen)

This is an early offense used by Indiana Pacers Coach Larry Brown. It is created to get center Rik Smits a post-up position or to pop point guard Mark Jackson to the top to look for an opening after a weak side down screen.

In Figure 3, 1 (Jackson) passes to 2 and begins the give-and-go cut to the basket. Player 1 stops and moves up the lane to set a back screen for 5 (Smits). Player 2 looks to make the pass to 5 in the post after a cut off the back screen.

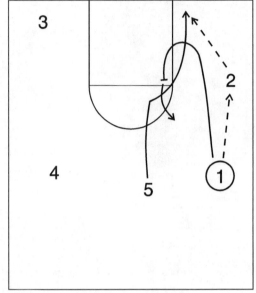

Figure 3

In Figure 4, if the pass into the post is denied, then 1 pops out to the top after setting his screen. Player 2 passes to 1. Player 1 looks for a possible high-low pass inside to 5 or to the weak side for a pass to 3 cutting off the screen from 4. Player 3 looks for a shot, drive or pass into the post to 4. (Possible option: 3 also can be used to set the back screen for 4 on the weak side to give the play a different look.)

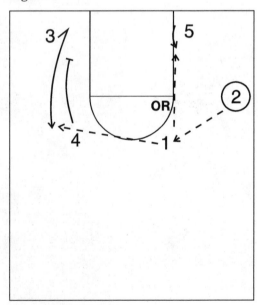

Figure 4

Indiana Head Coach Larry Brown

Indiana's Quick (2-5 Back Screen)

Another wrinkle to the quick set used by Indiana's Larry Brown is run to utilize 2-man Reggie Miller and center Rik Smits.

Instead of passing to 2 (Figure 3), in Figure 5, 1 dribbles to the right wing. 2 (Miller) starts toward the basket and cuts up the lane to set a back screen for 5 (Smits). Player 1 looks to pass to 5 in the post.

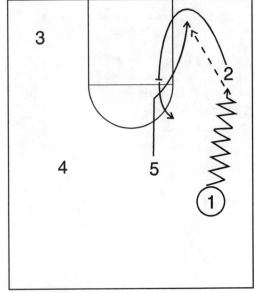

Figure 5

In Figure 6, if the post pass is denied, 1 passes to 2 at the top after he has set his back screen. Player 2 looks for a high-low pass to 5, the shot or drive, or passes to 4, cutting off 3's back screen on the weak side. If those options are denied, 2 looks to 3 who has popped out to the wing for a shot or post feed to 4.

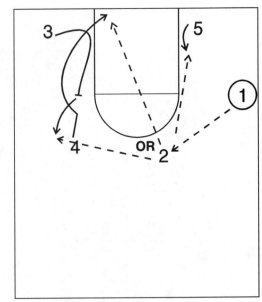

Figure 6

Quick Drag

This play was used by Bob Hill when he was coaching at Indiana as part of his early offense to utilize point guard Vern Fleming, forward Detlef Schrempf and shooting guard Reggie Miller.

In Figure 7, 1 (Fleming) drives off a late "drag" screen and roll set by 4 (Schrempf). As the screen and roll takes place, 2 (Miller) cuts off the baseline staggered screens set by 3 and 5. Player 3 sets a back screen for 4 and looks for a possible lob pass from 1 if the pass to 2 is denied.

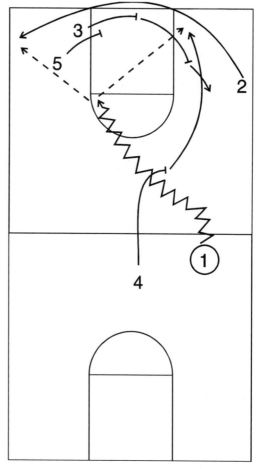

Figure 7

Chapter 2
SCREEN AND ROLL PLAYS

Sideline Screen and Roll Play (with spot ups)

A screen and roll play that Phoenix's Paul Westphal likes to use is run by a number of teams. The Suns take advantage of the quickness of point guard Kevin Johnson and the shooting range of Dan Majerle. Chuck Daly used it in Detroit with Isiah Thomas and Joe Dumars. In New Jersey, Daly used it on the opposite side of the floor since Kenny Anderson is left handed, and he has the opportunity to come off the screen and roll with his strong hand.

In Figure 8, 1 (Johnson) sets up his defender by dribbling the ball at least to the free throw line extended. (Player 1 can take the ball deeper with 4 adjusting his screening angle.) Player 1 runs a screen and roll with 4. Player 5 dives to the right box. Player 1 has several options: a) he can look to shoot or drive, b) he can pass to 4 on the roll, or c) swing the ball back to 2 (Majerle). If 2 doesn't have a shot, he can feed the ball to 3 in the corner for a shot or post feed to 5.

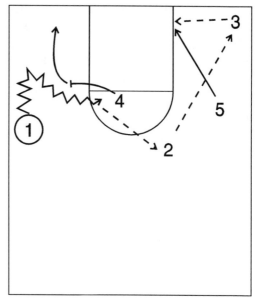

Figure 8

Phoenix's Side Screen and Roll (with weak side screen)

Another version of the sideline screen and roll play features a weak side screen. Phoenix uses it with Kevin Johnson and Charles Barkley running the screen and roll and Dan Majerle cutting for a three-pointer.

In Figure 9, 1 (Johnson) dribbles on the right side, penetrating to the free throw line extended. Player 4 (Barkley) runs a screen and roll with 1. If 1 has a shot or can continue his drive to the basket, he takes it. If 4 is open on the roll, 1 passes to 4. On the weak side, 2 cuts off a screen from 5, and 1 can pass to 2 (Majerle) for a three-point shot.

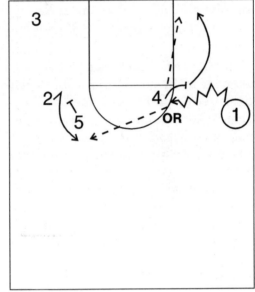

Figure 9

Kevin Johnson

Phoenix's Screen and Roll to Flare

Phoenix Suns Coach Paul Westphal likes to use this screen and roll play to free Dan Majerle or Danny Ainge for a jump shot.

In Figure 10, 1 and 2 (Majerle or Ainge) execute a screen and roll with the screen set above the left elbow of the lane. Player 3 cuts along the baseline off 5, moving toward the ball. After 2 sets the screen, he flares off the back screen set by 4. All the action moving left is a decoy as 1 throws back to 2 for a jump shot. Player 1 can also look to 3 if the pass to 2 is denied.

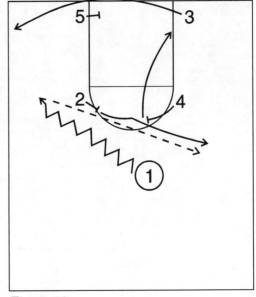

Figure 10

Paul Westphal and Charles Barkley

San Antonio's Side Screen and Roll (with weak side triple stack)

When John Lucas was coaching the San Antonio Spurs, he liked to use the screen and roll with guard Vinnie Del Negro and center David Robinson.

In Figure 11, 1 (Del Negro) runs a screen and roll with 5 (Robinson). Player 1 looks for the shot or passes to 5 on the roll. On the weak side, 2 cuts to the top out of a triple stack after using screens from 3 and 4. Player 1 also can look to 2 for the jump shot. If 2 does not have a scoring opportunity, he now has a triangle formed on the left side with 3 cutting to the corner. Players 2 and 3 can work with 4 for a possible post-up.

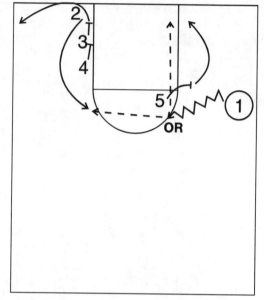

Figure 11

Orlando's High Screen and Roll Play

Orlando Magic Coach Brian Hill likes to use the middle of the floor to capitalize on the ball handling of point guard Anfernee Hardaway and the inside moves of center Shaquille O'Neal in his version of the screen and roll. Washington Bullets Coach Jim Lynam also uses this action by running the screen and roll with point guard Scott Skiles and center Gheorghe Muresan and bringing Juwan Howard to the top for jump shots.

In Figure 12, 1 (Hardaway) and 5 (O'Neal) run a screen and roll at the top of the key. Player 1 tries to turn the corner, looking for the shot or drive. His passing options include: a) passing to 5 on his roll to the basket, b) passing to 2 in the corner if 2's defender helps on 1, or c) passing back to 4 who flashes high, opening up the lane for 5's roll.

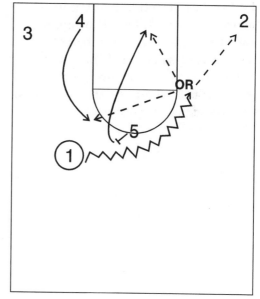

Figure 12

Screen and Roll Action for 3-Man

Another screen and roll play used by Chicago's Phil Jackson gets small forward Scottie Pippen in position to show off his talents.

In Figure 13, 1 passes to 3 (Pippen) on the wing and cuts through off screens from 2 and 4 on the weak side. Player 5 moves to set a screen for 3. Player 3 drives off 5, looking for these options, based on how the screen and roll is defended: a) shoot, b) drive for a shot or pass to 2 or 4 if their defender helps out, c) pass to 5 on the roll, or d) pass out to 1 who has cut off the weak side screens.

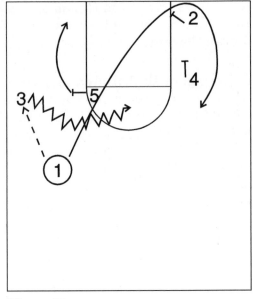

Figure 13

Chicago Head Coach Phil Jackson

Golden State's Screen and Roll (out of the post)

Former Golden State Warriors Coach Don Nelson liked to run this screen and roll action out of a turn-out look. He would run it with any of his post-up players and any of his perimeter players to give it several different looks over the course of a game.

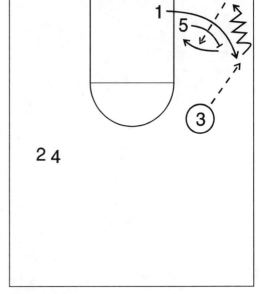

In Figure 14, the play is designed to use the point guard (Tim Hardaway or Keith Jennings) and center (Chris Gatling or Victor Alexander).

Player 1 (Hardaway) turns out off 5 (Gatling) with 3 passing to 1. The set looks like a turn-out to post-up play which catches teams off guard as 5 quickly leaves the post to set a ball screen on 1's defender. Player 1 drives to the outside on the screen and roll action and looks to pass to 5 rolling to the basket.

Figure 14

Chapter 3
POST-UP PLAYS

Houston's Turn-Out

Hakeem Olajuwon was named Most Valuable Player of the NBA in 1993-94. He helped lead the Houston Rockets to the NBA championship. One of the Rockets' most used plays for freeing Olajuwon in the post was conceived by Rockets Coach Rudy Tomjanovich.

This simple set is designed to take advantage of a great post-up player with other offensive options created for his teammates according to how the defense double-teams the post. A key to Houston's success with this set is that the Rockets have excellent perimeter shooters and maintain good spacing to stretch out the defense. These diagrams demonstrate how to create passing options out of a variety of post double-teams.

In Figure 15, 3 (or can be the 2-man) turns out off 5 and receives a pass from 1. Player 3 feeds 5 (Olajuwon) and slides to the corner. (If 3 is not a good shooter, he may cut through to the opposite corner.) This simple post feed allows 5 to work inside for his shot. If the posted player commands a double-team from the defense, 5 must be able to pass to a teammate who has cut to the basket or spotted up for a jump shot. If no double-team occurs, 5 works for his shot in the post.

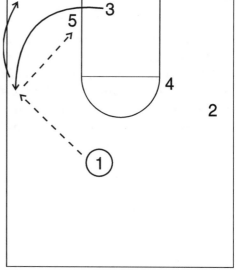

Figure 15

In Figure 16, if 3's defender double-teams the post, 5 should kick the ball out for a shot for 3. Player 3 can make the return pass to 5 as his defender recovers. Player 4 goes to the offensive board.

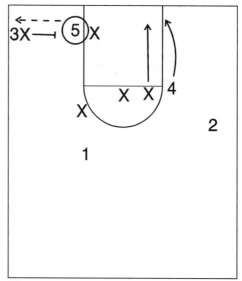

Figure 16

31

In Figure 17, if the double-team comes from 1's defender, 5 passes out to 1. Player 4 must be honored cutting to the weak side board. This forces 2's defender to rotate to 1. If he arrives in time to stop 1's shot or drive, 1 swings to 2 for a shot.

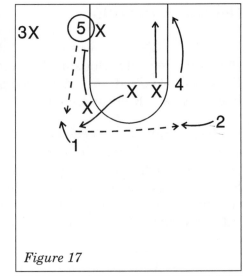

Figure 17

In Figure 18, if 5 is double-teamed by 4's defender, 4 cuts hard to the basket for a pass from 5. This will force 2's defender to guard 4. If the pass to 4 is denied, 5 looks to 2 spotting up for the jump shot at the top of the key.

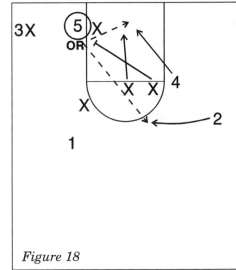

Figure 18

And finally, in Figure 19, if 2's defender double-teams 5, 4 cuts to the basket, again forcing his defender to make a decision whether to guard 2 or 4. Normally, he will be forced to stop the more dangerous basket cut, freeing 2 on the perimeter. If 1's defender slides over to play 2, 5 can pass to 1, who moves to create better spacing.

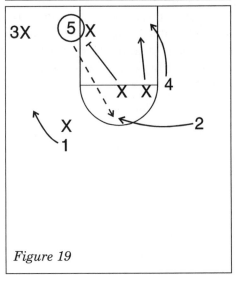

Figure 19

Lakers' Post 5-Man

Former Los Angeles Lakers Coach Randy Pfund had great success mixing in a post-feed to center Vlade Divac with two different cutting actions by point guard Sedale Threatt on the pass. He would use this action after running post-feeds for Divac to make his move inside with the point guard either spotting up or cutting through to the weak side. When the Lakers were in a "crunch" situation, you could expect either of these actions.

In Figure 20, 1 (Threatt) passes to 5 (Divac), sets up his defender and cuts hard to the outside of 5 for a handoff. Player 5 pivots (careful to avoid an offensive foul) and screens 1's defender. Player 1 runs his defender into 5 and comes off the handoff for a quick baseline jump shot. Player 2 cuts off 4's screen at the top to give another passing option if 1 is stopped.

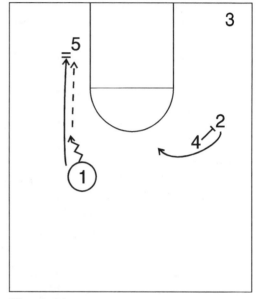

Figure 20

In Figure 21, 1 passes to 5 in the post. Instead of cutting for the handoff, 1 cuts inside of 5 to set a post screen and roll. Player 5 dribbles into the lane off 1's tail for a lay-up or hook shot. Player 1 cuts to the corner after setting a screen in the post. Players 2, 3 and 4 remain on the outside to create space for 5's drive. Divac uses a quick dribble into the lane and is ready to pass out to the spot-up players on the perimeter if their defenders help.

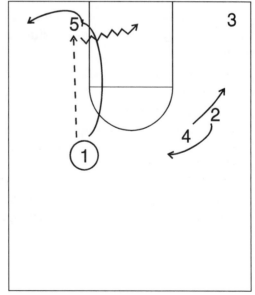

Figure 21

Utah's Back Pick

Utah Jazz Coach Jerry Sloan has one of the best power forwards in the league in Karl Malone. This is one of his favorite plays to free Malone in the post.

In Figure 22, 1 dribbles the ball to the wing as 2 sets a diagonal back screen for 4 (Malone). Player 4 works off 2 to post-up on the left box. Players 3 and 5 are lined up away from the play, but are ready to react to double-teams with 5 prepared to crash the board. Player 2 pops to the top after setting the screen to create even more space for 4 to work.

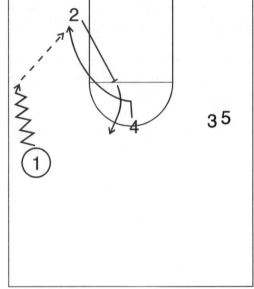

Figure 22

In Figure 23, if the pass to 4 from 1 is denied, 1 passes to 2 at the top of the key. 4 seals his defender and 2 looks for a high-low feed into the post. Player 5 holds his position and cuts to the board only after the pass inside is made.

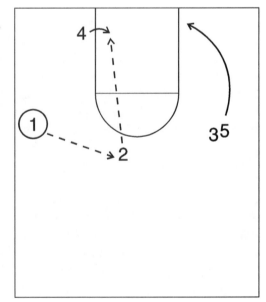

Figure 23

Karl Malone

Curl to Post-Up or Isolation

This action can be run to post-up or isolate any position. Coach Bob Weiss liked to use this play for Dominique Wilkins both at Atlanta and Los Angeles. Former Golden State Warriors Coach Don Nelson liked to utilize this curl action to attack the opponent's weakest defender.

In Figure 24, 2 curls tightly off 3 (Wilkins), trying to bump 3's defender to free 3 for a post-up or pop out for an isolation. When 3 pops out, 1 passes to 3 and slides away to give him room for a one-on-one play. Player 2 cuts to the corner and 4 and 5 remain high to create space for 3's one-on-one move. If any defender runs to double-team 3, the offensive player cuts behind him to the basket.

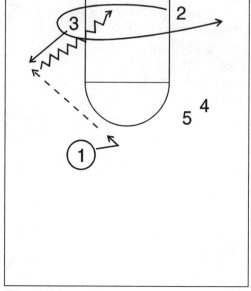

Figure 24

In Figure 25, if 3 is forced to pass out to 1, 5 and 4 double screen for 2. Player 2 catches the pass looking for an immediate shot, or passes to 4 cutting to the post. Player 5 creates space by moving to the opposite box.

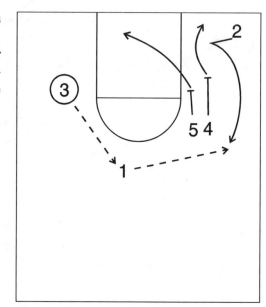

Figure 25

In Figure 26, if 3 has an advantage over his defender in the post, he can hold a position on the block and 1 passes to him inside after dribbling the ball to the wing to adjust the passing angle.

Coaches should adjust this set, based on what their 3-man does better (facing the basket or posting up) and whether or not he has an advantage in the post or out on the court against his defender.

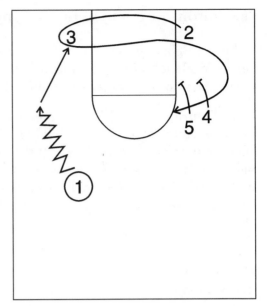

Figure 26

San Antonio's Post-Up for Robinson

David Robinson led the NBA in scoring in 1993-94. Former San Antonio Spurs Coach John Lucas had to devise several ways to get Robinson the ball in scoring positions. This was one of the Spurs' most successful plays.

In Figure 27, 5 (Robinson) screens down for 2 and posts up on the left box. Player 1 passes to 2 and flares off the back screen from 4 who now spots up at the top. The first option is 2 passing to 5 in the post.

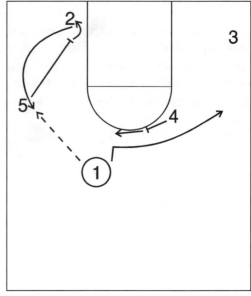

Figure 27

In Figure 28, if the pass into the post is denied, 2 passes to 4 at the top who swings the ball quickly to 1. As the pass is made to 1, 3 cuts to set a cross screen for 5. Player 1 looks for a pass to 5 on the right box or to the top to 3 who cuts off 4's screen on "screen the screener" action.

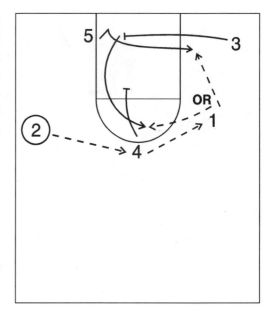

Figure 28

David Robinson

Minnesota's Cross Screen Reverse

Defensively, teams will often switch on cross screens. Against teams that usually switch, former Minnesota Timberwolves Coach Sidney Lowe used this play to post-up an unusually strong 3-man, Chuck Person. And Coach Bob Hill still uses this same action for Person at San Antonio.

In Figure 29, 3 (Person) sets a cross screen for 2 who cuts to the baseline side of 3 to the corner. On the switch, 3 seals his defender and tries to post him in front of the basket. 1 passes to 3. Player 1 also can pass to 2 in the corner who can then pass to 3 in the post. 5 and 4 stay high to give 3 room to maneuver inside.

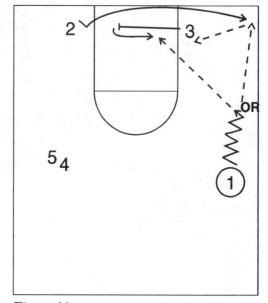

Figure 29

Chapter 4
FIST SET

Fist Play (Baseline Staggered Screens)

This action was best used by Chuck Daly when he was coaching in Detroit. He ran it time and time again for his trio of guards — Isiah Thomas, Joe Dumars and Vinnie Johnson.

In Figure 30, 2 cuts off the baseline staggered screens set by 3 and 5. Player 1 passes to 2 and slides away so if his defender helps on 2, he can spot up for a return pass. 3 pops off a screen from 4 after setting his screen for 2. This gives 1 the option of passing to 3 if 2 is covered. (As 2 is running around the screens, he must read how the defender is playing him. If his defender follows him off the screens, he curls off the last screen. If his defender cheats over the top of the screen, he should fade to the corner.) When 2 receives the pass, his options are: a) shoot, b) drive, c) pass to 5 in the post, or, d) pass to 1 if his defender drops off to help. If 5 isn't open, 5 can cross screen for 4, allowing 4 to post-up, or 5 can pop out of the post for a screen and roll with 2.

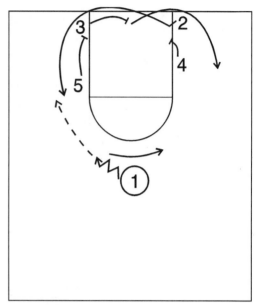

Figure 30

Fist Play Counter

One way to defend the Fist Play is by switching the 2 and 3 men. This counter is designed to attack this type of defensive maneuver.

In Figure 31, 3 fakes the screen on 2 and curls off 5, continuing to the opposite wing. Player 2 follows hard out the same side, working to beat his defender off the screen by 5. His defender will be anticipating a switch onto 3 and if executed properly, the defender will not be in a position to defend 2.

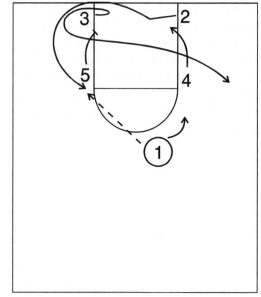

Figure 31

Fist Baseline Screen for Big Man

Chuck Daly liked to run this play for center Bill Laimbeer to take advantage of his outside shooting ability. It can be run for the 5 or 4, whichever is a good shooter facing the basket.

In Figure 32, 5 sets the first baseline staggered screen for 2, followed by 3. This decoy action looks like the play is designed to free 2 for a shot. After setting the screen, 5 pops off a screen from 4. Player 1 wheels back and delivers the pass to 5 (Laimbeer) for the shot.

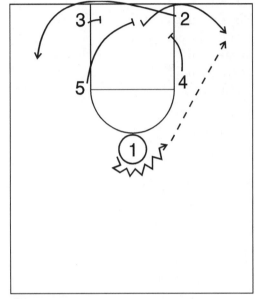

Figure 32

Fist Action to Post 3-Man

Seattle Sonics Coach George Karl uses this decoy action to post-up his 3-man, Detlef Schrempf.

In Figure 33, 2 cuts off staggered screens set by 3 (Schrempf) and 4. Player 5 pops out for a pass from 1 instead of screening for 3. Player 1 passes to 5 as 3 establishes post-up position on the right box. Player 5 passes to 3.

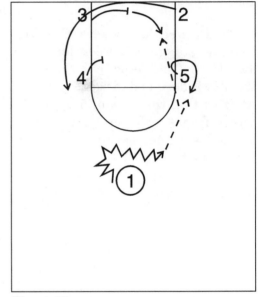

Figure 33

Seattle Head Coach George Karl

Chapter 5
HAWK SET

Hawk Set (Basic)

The Hawk Set is used in various forms by about a dozen teams. The name comes from the original play used by the Atlanta Hawks several years ago. Since then, teams have added option after option, thus creating a whole set of plays. Today, Houston Rockets Coach Rudy Tomjanovich is among the coaches who use it frequently.

In the basic action, in Figure 34, 1 penetrates to the wing as 2 rubs off 4 to a post-up position on the right box. Player 1 can pass to 2 or to 4 who pops out after 2's rub. This is a good action to post up a 2-man who can dominate his defender in the low post. (Examples: Todd Day of the Milwaukee Bucks and Bryant Stith of the Denver Nuggets.)

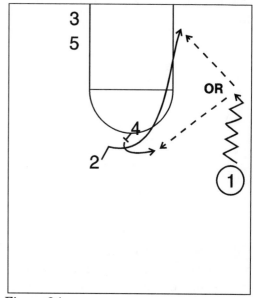

Figure 34

In Figure 35, if the pass goes to 4, 3 pops off 5, looking for a pass. Player 4 passes to 3 and sets a screen for 2. 3 has the following options: a) shoot, b) drive, c) pass to 5 in the post, or d) pass to 2 off 4's screen. (In Houston's attack, the swing pass is to forward Robert Horry, looking to pass to center Hakeem Olajuwon in the post.)

If 2 receives the pass, he looks for the shot. If he doesn't have a shot, he can swing it to 1 who looks to pass to 4 in the post.

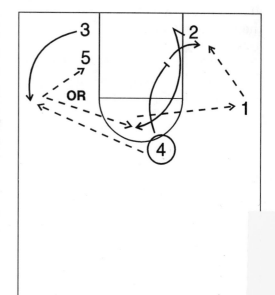

Figure 35

Hawk Set (2 off Baseline Stagger Screens)

In Figure 36, 2 rubs off 4 and cuts off the staggered screens set by 3 and 5. Player 1 passes to 4 who pops out. 4 looks to 2 as his first option. His second look is to 3 who slides in front of the basket if his defender helps on 2's cut.

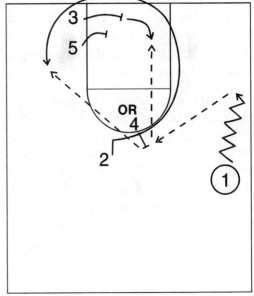

Figure 36

In Figure 37, when 2 catches the ball on the wing, he has the following options: a) shoot, b) drive, c) pass to 5 in the post, d) throw a lob pass to 4 after he cuts off a back screen from 3, or e) pass to 3 who pops out after setting the back screen for 4.

It also is possible to swing the ball from 3 to 1 for a post pass to 4, an action shown in Figure 35.

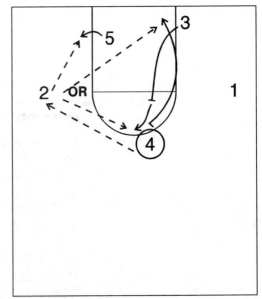

Figure 37

Houston Head Coach Rudy Tomjanovich

Hawk Set (Screen and Roll Option)

In Figure 38, after 2 rubs off 4, 2 cuts off a double screen from 3 and 5 on the baseline. Player 4 moves to set a screen and roll action with 1. Player 1 drives off 4's screen, looking for the following options: a) shoot, b) drive, c) pass to 2, or d) pass to 4 on the roll. (It is important for 3 and 5 to hold the double screen on the opposite lane line to create space for the roll by 4.)

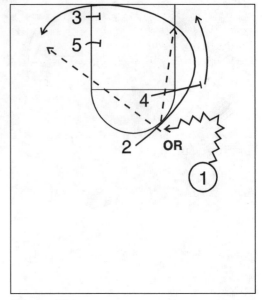

Figure 38

Hawk Set (Cross Screen to "Screen the Screener" Action)

In Figure 39, 2 rubs off 4 and sets a cross screen for 5 who cuts high or low off the screen into the post on the right box. Player 3 pops out to the wing. Player 4 screens down for 2 to send him to the top on the "screen the screener" action. Player 1 looks to pass to 5 in the post or to 2 at the top of the key for a jump shot.

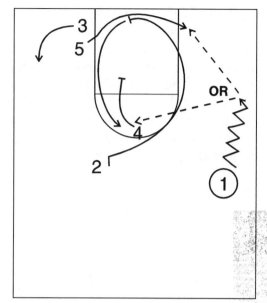

Figure 39

In Figure 40, if 2 does not have an open shot, he can swing to 3 who looks to 4 cutting to the post.

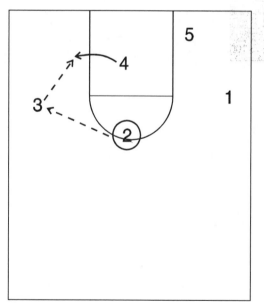

Figure 40

Hawk Set (Reverse "Screen the Screener" Action)

In Figure 41, after 2 rubs off 4, 4 sets a diagonal down screen for 5, bringing him to the top (this is a good option if the center is a good shooter facing the basket). Player 2 sets a screen for 4, bringing him to a post-up position on the right box. Player 1 looks to pass to 5 in the high post or to 4 cutting to the post off a screen from 2.

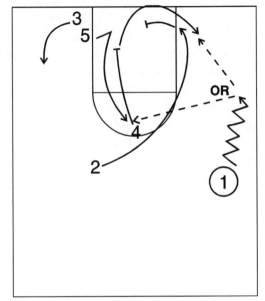

Figure 41

Chapter 6
ZIPPER SET

Zipper Set (Basic)

Like the Hawk Set, the Zipper Set is used by a number of NBA teams with a variety of options. In the New York Knicks' Zipper Set, Coach Pat Riley likes to post-up Patrick Ewing on the left box. The Milwaukee Bucks' Mike Dunleavy runs the zipper with a screen and roll on the top. The Indiana Pacers' Larry Brown likes to zipper Reggie Miller to the top and set a back screen for him so that he can flare for a three-point shot.

In the basic action in Figure 42, 1 dribbles to the wing as 4 sets a screen for 2 moving directly up the lane line. (Player 2 can cut to top off either side of 4, depending on how he is being defended.) Player 1 passes to 2 at the top. As 2 catches the ball, 5 down screens for 3 on the weak side. Player 2 passes to 3. Options for 3 are: a) shoot, b) drive, or c) pass to 5 in the post.

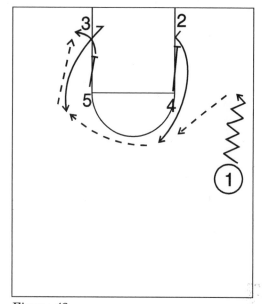

Figure 42

Zipper Set (With Screen and Roll)

In Figure 43, 1 dribbles to the wing and 4 down screens for 2 on the zipper action. 1 passes to 2. As 2 catches the ball, 5 moves to begin the screen and roll action. Player 3 clears to the right corner. Player 2 dribbles off 5 looking for the shot or pass to 5 on the roll to the basket.

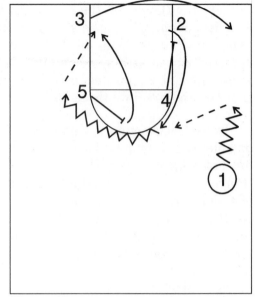

Figure 43

New York Head Coach Pat Riley

Zipper Set (With Back Screen Flare)

Indiana Pacers Coach Larry Brown will use center Rik Smits to bring 2-man Reggie Miller to the top on the zipper action.

In Figure 44, 2 (Miller) uses the screen from 5 (Smits) to go to the top. He hesitates at the top, then cuts off a back screen from 4 and flares for a skip pass from 1 and a three-point shot.

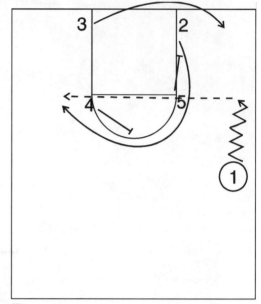

Figure 44

Reggie Miller

Zipper Drive

The Houston Rockets will use zipper action to set-up a quick drive for shooting guard Vernon Maxwell.

In Figure 45, 1 dribbles the ball to the wing as 2 (Maxwell) zippers to the top. Player 4 clears to the ball side corner. Player 2 looks to drive right on the catch. Player 3 flows to the open area on the right and if his defender helps on 2, 3 will be open for the spot-up jump shot.

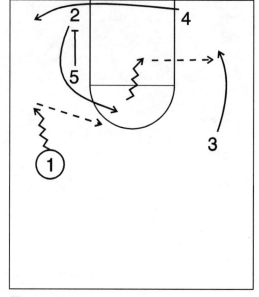

Figure 45

Zipper to Isolation

Detroit Pistons Coach Don Chaney runs this action for shooting guard Joe Dumars to create a one-on-one isolation for him off the zipper set.

In Figure 46, the zipper action is run in the normal manner, with the player to be used in the isolation lined up on the weak side. Player 1 dribbles to the opposite side of the floor from 2 (Dumars) and passes to 3, cutting off 4. As 3 catches the pass, 5 down screens for 2 and clears out, creating a one-on-one situation.

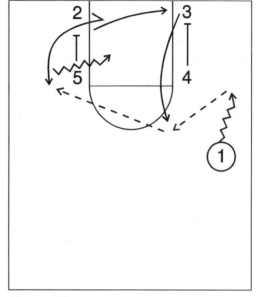

Figure 46

Chapter 7
COMBINATION PLAYS

New York's Baseline Cross

New York Knicks Coach Pat Riley likes to take advantage of the post-up abilities of his small forwards Charles Smith and Anthony Mason. He runs into this action by pushing the ball hard up the sideline.

In Figure 47, 1 drives to the free throw line extended. Player 2 sets a cross screen for 3 (Smith or Mason), bringing him to the right box. (In Riley's Lakers days, this was James Worthy posting up or cutting to the basket on the left side for a lob pass from Magic Johnson if his defender cheated over the screen.)

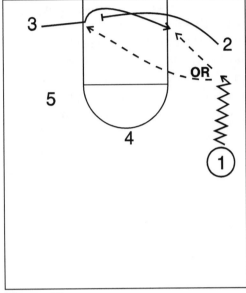

Figure 47

In Figure 48, if the pass to 3 is denied, 1 passes to 4 at the top of the key. Player 5 down screens for 2 on the weak side. 4 passes to 2 who looks for a shot, drive or pass into the post to 5. (This action results in John Starks feeding Patrick Ewing.)

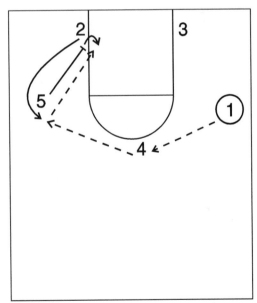

Figure 48

69

Baseline Cross with Double Down

This play is used often in Miami and Atlanta. Former Heat Coach Kevin Loughery liked to use it to get the ball into the post or a jump shot for Glen Rice; Hawks Coach Lenny Wilkens uses it to free Craig Ehlo on the perimeter.

In Figure 49, 1 dribbles to the wing as 2 (Rice or Ehlo) sets a cross screen for 3. After setting the screen, 2 cuts hard to the top off a double screen by 5 and 4. Player 1 has the possibility of passing to 3 in the post or passing to 2 at the top of the key for a jump shot.

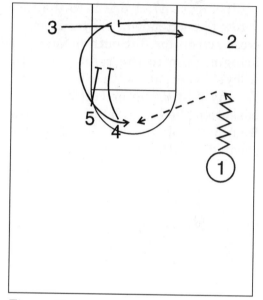

Figure 49

Craig Ehlo

Baseline Cross with Double Down (Counter)

To counter teams switching the previous 2-3 cross screen or cheating off 3 toward the right box, this counter play is used.

In Figure 50, 3 fakes coming across the lane and cuts hard off 5 and 4 at the top. Player 1 can pass to 3 at the top for a shot, or 3 can curl the double screen. Player 2 follows 3 and also cuts off the 5-4 double screen.

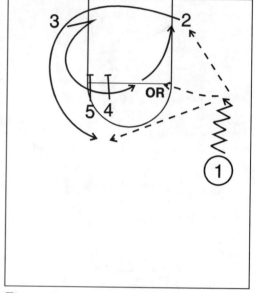

Figure 50

New Jersey's Screen and Roll Cross

Dream Team Coach Chuck Daly combined the screen and roll action at the elbow of the lane with a cross screen to a weak side down screen.

With the Detroit Pistons, Daly used Isiah Thomas (one of the best penetrators) and Bill Laimbeer (one of the league's best outside shooting big men). With the New Jersey Nets, Daly used point guard Kenny Anderson with power forward Derrick Coleman.

In Figure 51, 1 (Anderson) drives past a screen from 4 (Coleman). Player 1 looks for either 4 (popping out for a jump shot from the top of the key) or 3 (cutting to the post off 2's cross screen).

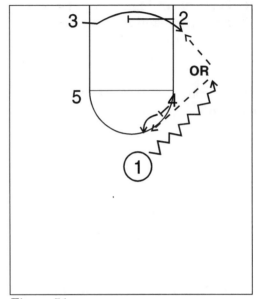

Figure 51

In Figure 52, if 4 does not have a shot, 5 down screens for 2. Player 4 passes to 2 who looks for a shot or passes to 5 in the post.

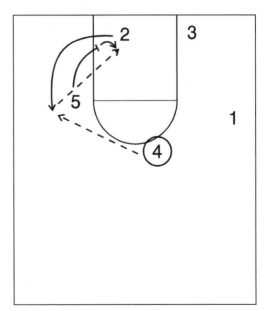

Figure 52

Dallas' Guards Through Set

Coach Dick Motta has used this action at every stop during his 23 years in the NBA, and it still is effective today with the Dallas Mavericks. Motta utilizes shooting guard Jim Jackson and point guard Jason Kidd to work off baseline screens. That frees small forward Jamal Mashburn to be used in the post.

This action is run with a two-guard front and can be started on either side of the court. In Figure 53, 1 passes to 4, runs a give-and-go cut and continues through to the opposite box. Player 2 cuts off 5 in the high post to the ball side box. Player 5 pops out for a pass from 4. Player 3 and 4 set down screens for 1 and 2.

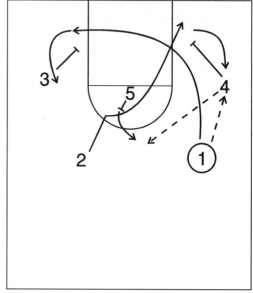

Figure 53

In Figure 54, 5 can pass to either side. In this case, he passes to 1 and screens away for 2. Player 1 (Kidd) looks for a shot, a post-feed to 3 (Mashburn), or to pass to 2 (Jackson) at the top.

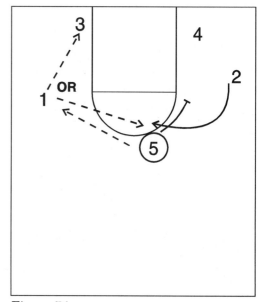

Figure 54

Dallas Head Coach Dick Motta

Split Post Action for 3-Man

Atlanta Hawks Coach Lenny Wilkens used this play originally for Dominique Wilkins, but when Wilkins was traded to the Los Angeles Clippers for Danny Manning, the Hawks ran it just as often for Manning.

In Figure 55, 1 passes to 5 in the high post and cuts off 5 to set a screen for 3 (Wilkins or Manning). Player 3 sets up his defender and cuts off 1. Player 5 looks to pass to 3, cutting off 1's screen. If the pass is denied, 3 keeps coming off 5 for a handoff. Player 4 screens down for 2 on the weak side to keep the other defenders occupied and to create a passing option for 3. Player 3 looks for a shot or drive or pass to 2.

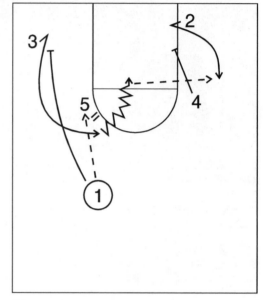

Figure 55

Atlanta Head Coach Lenny Wilkens

Chapter 8
FLEX ACTION

Flex Action

Flex action is used in the NBA to create player and ball movement. It is utilized to create continuity and to get all five offensive players involved in the action.

Often Sacramento Kings Coach Garry St. Jean or New York Knicks Coach Pat Riley will start games with this attack or switch to this offense when players are standing too much.

The flex has been run by a number of teams in the league and can be initiated in a variety of ways. The basic concept, however, involves flashing a player into the lane off a back screen after the ball has been reversed, then setting a down screen for the screener to bring him to the top. This creates the "screen the screener" action which is a popular NBA attack. The beauty of the flex is that continuity can be maintained, and the next ball reversal creates a "screen the screener" action to the opposite side.

The flex forces defenses to also move and to defend the down and back screens involved. It takes big defenders away from the basket and, if not defended properly, can force switches which the offense can take advantage of by attacking the mismatch.

This chapter will show the basics of the Sacramento and New York sets and also reveal additional flex options to keep defenses honest. The continuity of the NBA flex diagrammed shows a 4-man continuity, which creates a different look than the more common 5-man flex, which also will be diagrammed.

These are only the basic fundamentals of the flex. As defenses switch and cheat on screens, coaches must adjust to counter these defenses with basket cuts, bump backs, lob passes to the basket and post-ups of mismatches.

In the flex, 4 and 5 are interchangeable, as are 2 and 3. In Figure 56, 1 passes ahead to 2 and cuts through to the opposite corner. Player 4 (the first big man down the court) cuts to the ball side box. Player 5 fills the top and 3 cuts to the left wing. Player 1 can feed 4 in the post, but the flex action begins as the ball is reversed to 5.

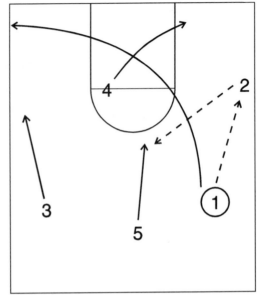

Figure 56

In Figure 57, 5 reverses the ball to 3, and 2 cuts into the lane off a back screen from 4. Player 2 must not cut off the screen until 3 has the ball and has made eye contact with 2. An early cut by 2 is wasted as 3 will not be able to deliver the ball because the defenders will have time to recover. Timing on all cuts is essential. After passing to 3, 5 sets a down screen for 4. Player 3 has the option of passing to 2 inside or passing to 4 at the top. Player 1 holds in the corner.

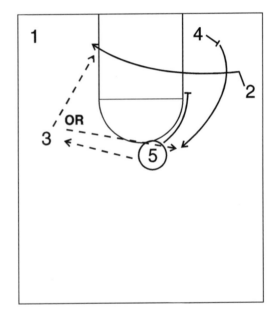

Figure 57

In Figure 58, continuity is created on a pass to 4. Player 5 cuts to the wing for a pass from 4, and 3 cuts off a back screen from 2. Again, timing is essential. "Screen the screener" action takes place as 5 sets a down screen for 2. Player 5 has the option of passing to 3 inside or passing to 2 at the top. With the NBA 24-second clock, this is all the continuity teams have time for. At other levels of the game, the ball can be reversed a greater number of times.

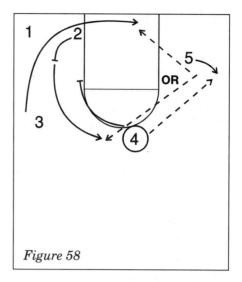

Figure 58

In Figure 59, 1 gets into the flex action by using a screen from the player on the wing (in this case, 4). The ball is reversed to 1, cutting off the screen, as 5 cuts off 3's back screen and 2 sets a down screen for 3. Player 4 holds in the corner. The wing can set a screen for the corner man and exchange positions at any time.

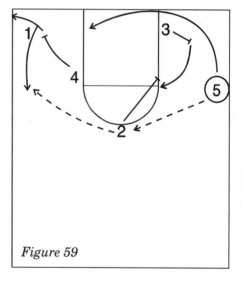

Figure 59

On the reversal in Figure 60, 1 cuts off 5's back screen and 3 sets a down screen for 5.

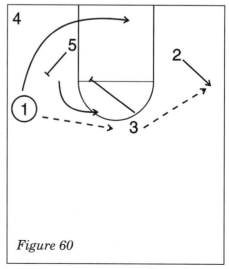

Figure 60

Flex to Lob

When defenders begin to play the back screen of the flex by going over the top of the screen, they can be set up for the lob pass. Coaches can use their best leaper between 2 and 3. The lob action can be run by reading the defense and reacting or by a specific call by the coach. Often this play can be set up after a time out, after the flex has been run a few times.

In Figure 61, on the pass to the top, the wing (in this case, 2) will set up his defender to go over the screen. The low post screener should step up higher to create space behind him for the lob cut. On the pass from 5 to 3, 2 cuts to the basket off a back screen from 4, and 3 throws a lob pass.

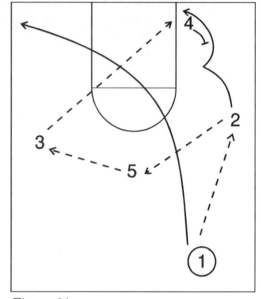

Figure 61

Flex to Corner Screen and Roll

The point guard also can be involved in the flex action by reversing the ball to the corner and running the player off a screen and roll.

In Figure 62, the flex begins as normal with the exception that 1 passes to 3 on the wing, instead of to 2. Player 3 reverses the ball to 5, who passes to 2. Player 3 cuts off the back screen from 4, and 5 sets a down screen for 4.

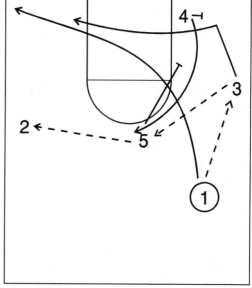

Figure 62

In Figure 63, 2 passes to 1 in the corner, instead of reversing the ball, and cuts off a back screen from 3. Player 1 looks for a possible lob pass to 2.

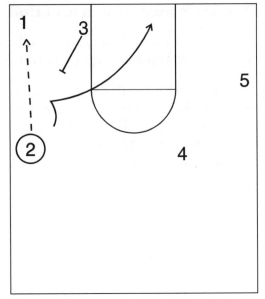

Figure 63

In Figure 64, if the lob pass is unavailable, 3 cuts to the corner to run a screen and roll with 1. Players 4, 5 and 2 spot up on the weak side or cut to the basket, depending on the defense's reaction to the screen and roll.

(This action began with an initial pass to 3, instead of 2, so that the screen and roll takes place with a bigger player setting the screen. If the initial pass is to 2, the 1-2 screen and roll will be easily switched by the defense.)

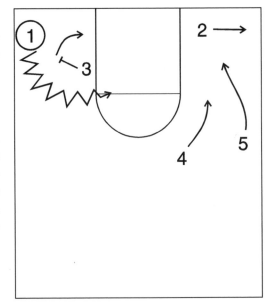

Figure 64

A 1-4 or 1-5 corner screen and roll can be set up by sliding the big man who posts up across the lane as the ball is reversed to the top. In Figure 65, 4 slides across and the "screen the screener" action does not take place as the corner screen and roll is the focus of the play. Player 3 passes to 1 in the corner and cuts off the back screen from 4, looking for the give and go action on the inside cut, instead of over the inside of the screen for the lob pass.

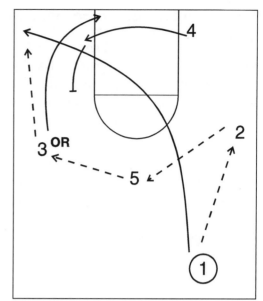

Figure 65

If the pass to 3 is not available, in Figure 66, 4 moves out to run a corner screen and roll with 1. Player 5 sets a screen for 2 on the weak side to occupy the defense and bring a shooter to the top. By sliding 4 across the lane, the screen and roll takes place with a bigger player and is more difficult to switch.

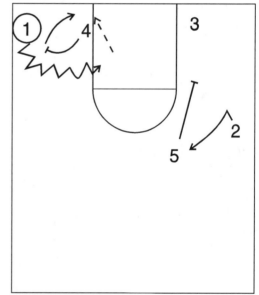

Figure 66

Flex with Staggered Screens for 2

This is a designated set play off the flex to create a scoring opportunity for the shooting guard. New York has had great success bringing John Starks off staggered screens for jump shots. After running the flex continuity a number of times, the shooting guard's defender will be focused on playing the back screen and flash across the lane. This will set him up to be picked off by screens set by 4 and 5.

In Figure 67, 1 passes to 2. Player 1 clears to the opposite corner, and 2 passes to 5 at the top. Player 2 cuts off a screen from 4 to the opposite box. Player 5 passes to 3.

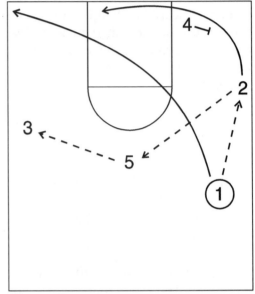

Figure 67

In Figure 68, 4 and 5 set staggered screens for 2 who returns to a spot on the wing. 3 passes to 2 (Starks) for the jump shot.

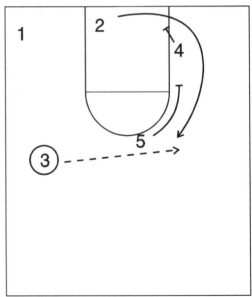

Figure 68

Flex with Quick Cross Screen to the Post

This action can be mixed in with the flex to create a quick hitting post-up for a good back-to-the-basket player. This action has been successful for the Indiana Pacers in getting center Rik Smits the ball inside. The Washington Bullets use point guard Scott Skiles to set a quick cross screen in the lane for power forwards Chris Webber and Juwan Howard.

In Figure 69, 1 passes to 2 on the wing and cuts through toward the weak side corner as in the normal flex. Player 1 quickly reverses himself and sets a cross screen for 5 as the ball is passed from 2 to 4 and reversed to 3. Player 3 feeds 5 (Smits) in the post.

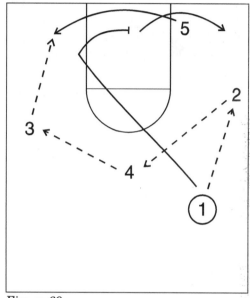

Figure 69

In Figure 70, the same play is run for a power forward (Webber or Howard). The player receiving the pass in the post should be the best post-up player on the team or a player who can attack a weaker defender in the post.

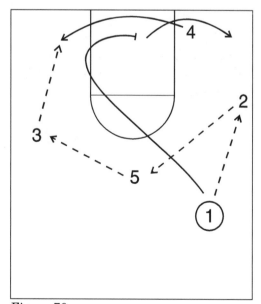

Figure 70

Flex with Quick Cross to "Screen the Screener"

The quick post action develops as in previous diagrams with the cross screen for 4. In Figure 71, after the ball is reversed to 3, the first look is to 4 in the post. If this pass is denied, 5 can set a down screen for 1 to bring him to the top for a possible jump shot on "screen the screener" action. Player 2 flows to the corner for good spacing.

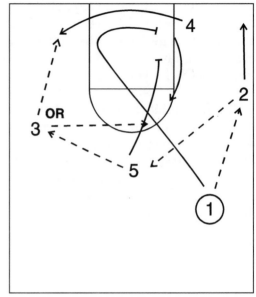

Figure 71

5-Man Flex Attack

The Washington Bullets under former Coach Wes Unseld used a 5-man flex which is used at all levels of basketball. This offense uses a two-guard front and the angle of the back screen and cut into the lane are different. Again, this offense creates player and ball movement and involves all five players. There are a number of ways to initiate this attack. The following diagrams illustrate one way to initiate the two-guard front, three along the baseline look of the 5-man flex. Shots in this offense will come in the lane off the baseline flex cut or at the elbow of the lane on the "screen the screener" action.

In Figure 72, 1 brings the ball up the left side and looks to reverse the ball to 2 who sets a back screen for 4 and pops out for a pass. Player 4 widens out to create space for the flex cut.

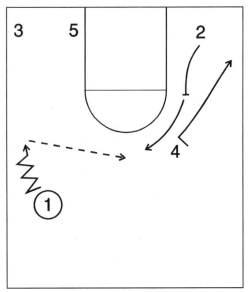

Figure 72

In Figure 73, 3 cuts off the back screen from 5, and 1 down screens for 5 on the "screen the screener" action.

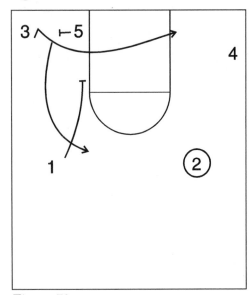

Figure 73

In Figure 74, continuity is maintained as 2 passes to 5, and 4 cuts off the back screen from 3. Player 1 widens out to create space, and 2 sets a down screen for 3.

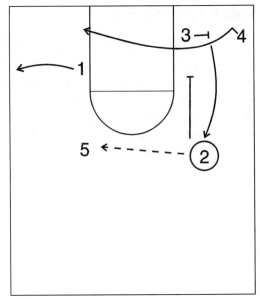

Figure 74

If a pass is thrown into the corner, there is a cross screen at the top. In Figure 75, 5 passes to 1 and screens for 3.

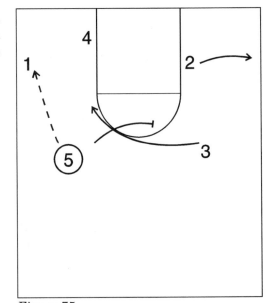

Figure 75

Flex "Hold" Option

On a "hold" call, the baseline flex cut does not take place as the ball is reversed to the corner. In Figure 76, 2 passes to 5. 3 and 4 maintain their positions ready to spot up or rebound as 5 passes to 1 and follows the pass to run a screen and roll action.

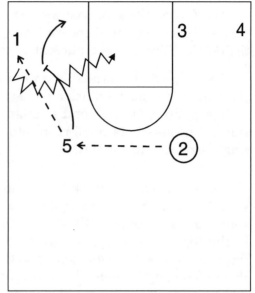

Figure 76

The Boston Slice

The Boston Slice incorporates some of the elements of the flex, but is a set play and does not afford the continuity of the flex. Used by many NBA teams, the Boston Slice was popularized by the Boston Celtics.

The slice can be formed in a number of different ways, but the object is to establish a low double stack on one side of the floor with a good shooter in the bottom position (1 or 2) and to align a slashing player (3) on the side of the stack. The slice cuts the 3-man into the lane off a double screen instead of a single screen as in the flex.

In Figure 77, the stack is formed with 1 and 5, as 1 passes to 3 on the wing and cuts under 5. Player 4 cuts to the top and is the reversal man. Player 3 passes to 4 who passes to 2. Player 3 sets up his defender and cuts into the lane off the 1-5 double screen, looking for a pass from 2.

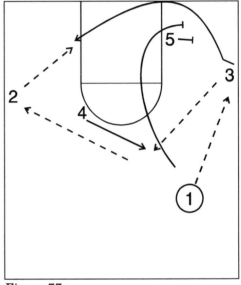

Figure 77

In Figure 78, if the pass to 3 is denied, 2 looks for a pass to 1, who cuts from the bottom of the stack off a down screen from 4. If the defender on 2 helps on the cut by 3, 1 will be open for the jump shot.

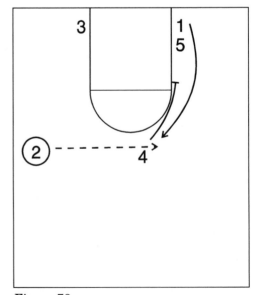

Figure 78

When the Washington Bullets used the slice under former Coach Wes Unseld, they wanted to set up shooting guard Rex Chapman for the jump shot.

In Figure 79, the Bullets got into the set with 2 and 5 forming the double screen on the left side. Player 4 sets up at the left elbow and 3 receives the pass on the left wing (a total overload formation). Player 1 passes to 3 and cuts to the opposite wing. Player 4 seals off his defender and pops out for a pass from 3.

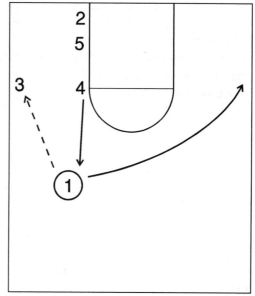

Figure 79

In Figure 80, 4 swings a pass to 1, and 3 cuts off the 2-5 double screen to the lane. Player 4 down screens for 2, bringing the preferred shooter (Chapman) to the top for the jump shot. Player 1 looks to 3 in the post or to 2 at the top.

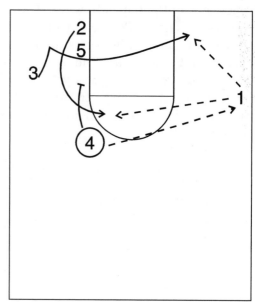

Figure 80

95

Boston Slice with Back Screen to Back Door

Other teams will align the 4-man on the opposite elbow of the low stack. In Figure 81, when 1 passes to 3, 4 sets a back screen for 1 and pops to the ball for the reversal pass. This action is effective when teams are overplaying the pass to the top.

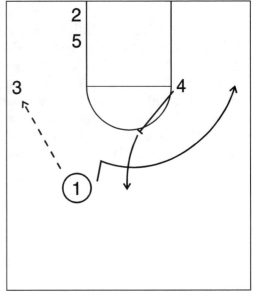

Figure 81

Some teams will work to deny the pass to 1 on the opposite wing. If this occurs, in Figure 82, 3 bumps back off the double screen and 1 sets up his defender on the overplay and back doors for a pass from 4. (3 always has the option to bump back off the double screen if his defender cheats into the lane.)

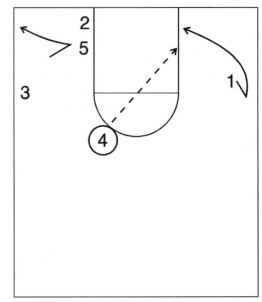

Figure 82

Chicago's Baseline Slice Cut

Chicago Bulls Coach Phil Jackson liked to use this play during the championship seasons when he had Horace Grant at power forward and Bill Cartwright at center.

In Figure 83, 2 down screens for 3 on the left side. Player 1 passes to 3. Player 4 (Grant) slices off 5's back screen into the lane. Player 3 looks to pass to 4 as the first option. Player 5 (Cartwright) ducks into the lane after 4 crosses for a possible pass from 3. If neither option is available, 3 passes back to 1, and 5 seals his defender to establish post position. 1 passes to 5.

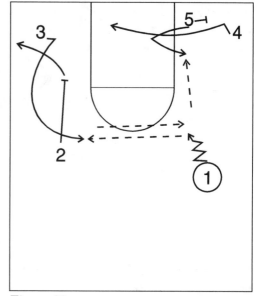

Figure 83

Chapter 9
THREE-POINT PLAYS

Step Up Play

Generally, three-point shot attempts are set-up with screen and roll actions, back screens with flares, setting single or staggered screens to free a shooter, weaves (dribble handoffs), or penetration and throw backs. Any of the screen and roll plays discussed in Chapter 3 can be adjusted to set-up a three-point shot. All that is required is for the screen to be set above the three-point line. The shot can be created for the dribbler moving off the screen or for the screener who rolls away from the basket. Three-point shots can be set-up from a side out-of-bounds situation or in the flow of play in a half court set or an Early Offense.

This is one of the most successful plays out of an Early Offense, run by a number of teams. San Antonio Spurs Coach Bob Hill uses it to free Sean Elliott or Chuck Person.

In Figure 84, 1 pushes the ball hard up the right side. He uses a screen set by 3 (Elliott or Person). Player 3 fades back after the screen, and 1 passes to 3 for the shot. On the weak side, 2 can cut off staggered screens by 4 and 5, giving 3 another option if he cannot get off the shot.

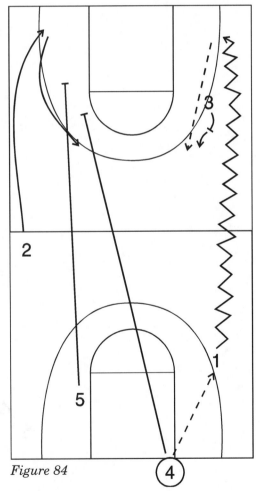

Figure 84

Triple Stagger for a 3

This is another play used by many teams off their early offense. It is used most effectively if a team has two outside threats. When Bob Hill was coaching the Indiana Pacers, he had great success with this play using Reggie Miller at 2 and Chuck Person at 3.

In Figure 85, 1 pushes the ball hard up the right side at 2. As 1 crosses half court, 2 cuts off three screens set by 3, 4 and 5. Player 1 passes back across the court to 2 looking for the shot.

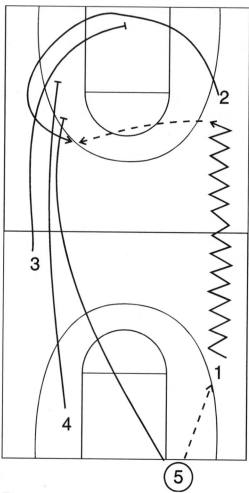

Figure 85

In Figure 86, if the shot for 2 is not open, 3 cuts to the corner off staggered screens set by 4 and 5. 2 looks to pass to 3. This action provides looks at three-point attempts by both 2 (Miller) and 3 (Person). The key to this play is for the 4 and 5 men to set good screens for both players.

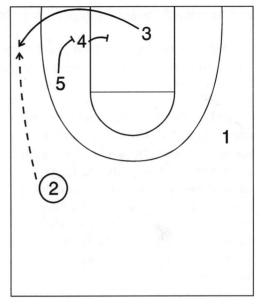

Figure 86

Milwaukee's Side Screen and Roll (with a flare)

Milwaukee Bucks Coach Mike Dunleavy likes to run his own version of the screen and roll play with a back screen flare for his shooting guard Todd Day on the weak side.

In Figure 87, 1 and 5 run the screen and roll, and 2 (Day) flares off 4 for a possible three-point shot. After setting the screen, 4 pops out high, spotting for a three-point attempt if his defender helps on 2. If 2 is not free for the shot, he looks quickly to 4 or penetrates, trying to draw help from 3's defender and kicks a pass out to 3, spotting up behind the three-point line.

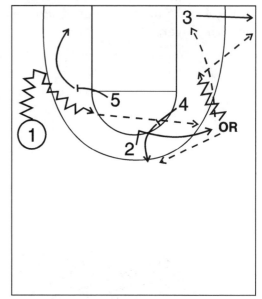

Figure 87

Milwaukee Head Coach Mike Dunleavy

Side Out of Bounds for a 3

A number of teams utilize this "X" play from the side out-of-bounds situation. Each team makes its own adjustments to fit its personnel, but the best example is the Detroit Pistons when Chuck Daly was the coach. Daly brought Isiah Thomas to the top for the initial look at a three-pointer, and then sent Joe Dumars off staggered screens as the second option.

In Figure 88, 4 begins the X action by cutting first off 5 to the left box. Player 2 (Dumars) follows, cutting over 5 to the right box. When 2 passes by, 5 sets a down screen for 1 (Thomas) in the middle of the lane. Player 3 passes to 1 at the top of the key for a possible three-point attempt.

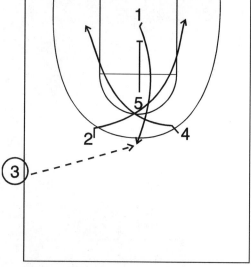

Figure 88

In Figure 89, if 1 does not have the shot, he looks to pass to 2, cutting off staggered screens from 4 and 3. Player 5 spots up on the right side, giving another passing option.

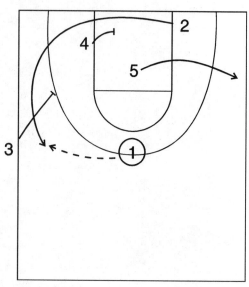

Figure 89

Isiah Thomas

Baseline Out of Bounds for a 3

Seattle Sonics Coach George Karl utilizes this play from under their own basket to create a three-point shot attempt for big man Sam Perkins. Coaches can adapt this play to create the shot for their best shooter. In the Sonics' case, it is tough for a center to chase down Perkins off staggered screens, and he usually gets off a good shot.

In Figure 90, 5 (Perkins) inbounds the ball to 1 who seals his defender and pops to the corner. Player 5 cuts to the top off triple staggered screens set by 2, 3 and 4. Player 1 passes to 5 at the top for the jump shot.

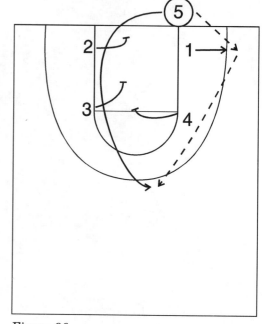

Figure 90

Chapter 10
OUT-OF-BOUNDS PLAYS

Los Angeles Clippers' Motion Play

When the Clippers had Dominique Wilkins (at 3) and Ron Harper (at 2), former Coach Bob Weiss used their explosive one-on-one skills on this sideline out-of-bounds play.

In Figure 91, 3 (Wilkins) passes to 5 who has popped out on the side. While 5 passes the ball to 4, 3 cuts off 2's (Harper) back screen into the lane. Player 4 looks to pass to 3 in the lane as 1 clears the area by popping out to the corner.

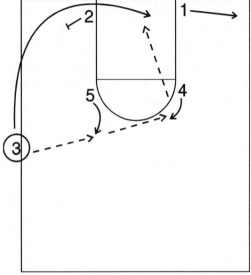

Figure 91

In Figure 92, if the pass to 3 is denied, 5 sets a screen for 2 to complete the "screen the screener" action as 4 passes to 2.

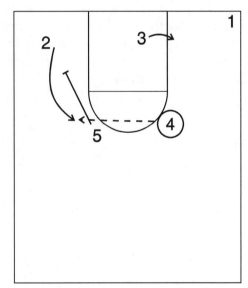

Figure 92

111

Seattle's Staggered Back Screen Play

Seattle Sonics Coach George Karl uses this sideline out-of-bounds play to free power forward Shawn Kemp in the post or get the ball into the hands of 2-man Kendall Gill.

In Figure 93, 1 inbounds the ball to 4 (Kemp) and cuts behind 4 for a handoff. Player 1 dribbles off 5's screen and roll as 4 cuts off a pair of staggered back screens from 3 and 2. 1 looks to feed 4 in the post.

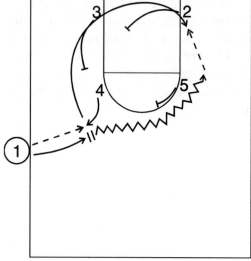

Figure 93

In Figure 94, if the pass to 4 is denied, 1 looks for 2 (Gill) who has cut off the screen from 5 (after setting the screen for 1, 5 rolls into the screen for 2 as 3 clears to the wing).

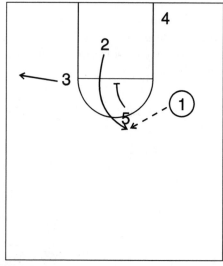

Figure 94

Kendall Gill

Chicago's Line to Staggered Down Screens

Chicago Bulls Coach Phil Jackson likes to run this sideline out-of-bounds play to get point guard B.J. Armstrong a jump shot or to initiate the Bulls' patented Triangle Offense.

In Figure 95, 3 inbounds to 2 who has popped out for the pass. Player 1 (Armstrong) cuts to the left box. Player 2 passes to 4 cutting to the ball at the right elbow of the lane, then runs behind 4 to the right wing. Player 5 moves to set the first screen for 1, and 3 positions himself for the second screen.

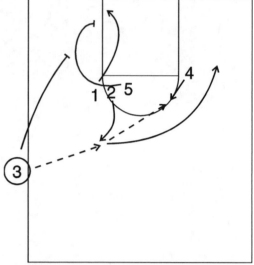

Figure 95

In Figure 96, 4 looks to pass to 1 (if he is open) after he has cut off the two staggered screens, or 4 can throw it back to 2. After passing to 2, 4 follows his pass to run a screen and roll play with 2.

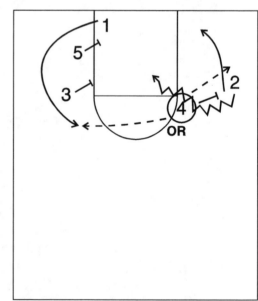

Figure 96

114

Atlanta's Baseline Triple

The Atlanta Hawks take advantage of 2-guard Craig Ehlo's abilities to use screens and hit the outside jump shot. Coach Lenny Wilkens runs Ehlo off a series of three screens to create an open jump shot from the wing.

In Figure 97, 3 inbounds to 2 who pops out to the corner. Player 5 screens for 1. Player 2 passes to 1, and 3 steps into the post.

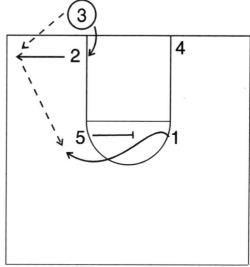

Figure 97

In Figure 98, 2 cuts off staggered screens by 3, 4 and 5. Player 1 can look for a quick post-up by 3 or pass to 2 (Ehlo) for the jump shot.

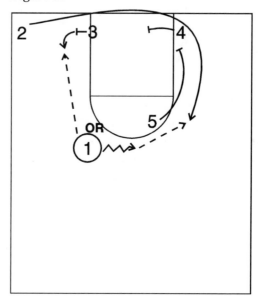

Figure 98

Sacramento's Baseline Play

Sacramento Kings Coach Garry St. Jean uses 2-man Mitch Richmond to curl to the ball and bring point guard Spud Webb to the corner off two staggered screens.

In Figure 99, 2 curls to the basket off 4 and 5. As soon as 2 curls, 4 and 5 set staggered screens for 1, who cuts to the corner. Player 3 looks first for 2 (Richmond), then to 1 (Webb) in the corner.

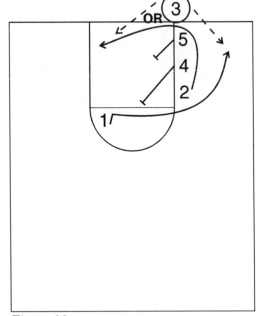

Figure 99

The Kings also have a variation of the same play. In Figure 100, 3 waits for 1 to clear to the corner, then looks to 4 who cuts off the screen from 5.

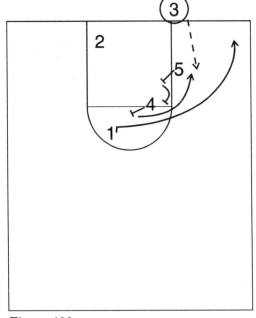

Figure 100

Houston's Baseline Cross

This play is similar to one utilized by the Chicago Bulls for a number of years. Chicago used Michael Jordan, Horace Grant and Bill Cartwright. It is just as effective when Houston Rockets Coach Rudy Tomjanovich uses it to get center Hakeem Olajuwon position in the post.

In Figure 101, 2 looks to inbound the ball on a possible lob to 3 or to 3 in the corner cutting off a screen from 4. 1 floats to the outside as a safety valve if the defense prevents 3 from getting free.

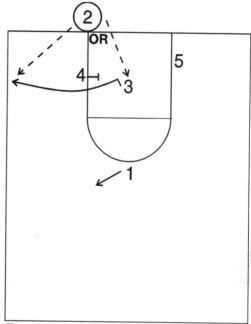

Figure 101

In Figure 102, once 3 has the ball, 2 clears out the lane by running away from the play. Player 3 looks for 5 (Olajuwon) in the low post after 5 uses a cross screen by 4.

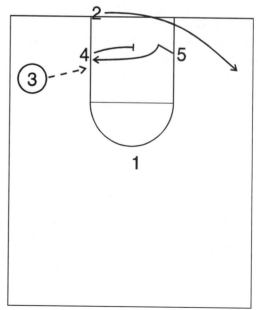

Figure 102

ABOUT THE AUTHORS

Bob Ociepka

Widely regarded as one of the best X's and O's scouts in the National Basketball Association, Bob Ociepka is currently an assistant coach with the Los Angeles Clippers.

As an advance scout, Ociepka has spent the past seven seasons diagramming every play that every team in the NBA runs. He joined the NBA as an assistant coach with the Indiana Pacers in 1989.

He has a unique perspective on the game of basketball after literally going from the bench of a high school team to the bench of an NBA squad in a week's time. He was a highly successful prep coach in Chicago for 19 years before joining the staff of the Pacers in mid-season.

Ociepka was a standout player at Quincy (Ill.) College before becoming a coach.

Dale Ratermann

After working 11 years for the athletic department at the University of Illinois, Dale Ratermann joined the front office staff of the Indiana Pacers in 1985. He is currently the Pacers' vice president of administration.

Ratermann has written several sports books.

Look for these great Masters Press Titles...

Basketball Inbound Attack
Tom Reiter

The most comprehensive, effective — and only — collection of inbound plays available!

128 pages - 7 x 10
ISBN 0-940279-60-6 - $12.95
diagrams - paper

Basketball Crosswords
Dale Ratermann

Includes word searches, photographs, retired jersey numbers and team histories for all 27 NBA teams.

192 pages - 7 x 10
ISBN 1-57028-004-5
b\w photos - paper

Coaching Basketball
Edited by Jerry Krause

A collection of more than 130 articles and essays by the game's leading coaches, covering every aspect of the game.

320 pages - 8 1/2 x 11
ISBN 0-940279-86-X - $19.95
diagrams - paper

**All Masters Press titles,
including those in the Spalding Sports Library,
are available at bookstores or by calling
(800) 722-2677.
Catalogs are available upon request.**